The God Really Loves You Book Series™ Presents:

GOD Really Loves You
and
He Gives You Special Gifts!

**Written and Illustrated
by Wendy Nelson**

God Really Loves You Book Series™ presents:

GOD Really Loves You
and He Gives You Special Gifts!

Text Copyright ©2024 by Wendy Nelson
Artwork Copyright ©2024 by Wendy Nelson

Published by MediaTek Grafx
POB 62, Bonnieville, Kentucky, 42713

ISBN 979-8-3302-6157-4

Design and production by MediaTek Grafx, Bonnieville, Kentucky
Special thanks to Joan Swan for loving review, encouragement and advice

The Publisher has made every effort to avoid errors or omissions. Opinions, stories, and themes are intended for entertainment, motivation for research and future study. This book includes content that is non-fiction.

All Scripture quotations are from the The Holy Bible, King James Version, Pradis Software Rel 02.04.03, Built with Conform Version 5.00.0051, Version 5.1.50 Copyright ©2002 The Zondervan Corporation All Rights Reserved.

All rights reserved. This Publication may not be reproduced in whole or in part, stored or transmitted by any means. Media may use small portions for reviews. Please request written permission from Publisher for any other reason.

Printed in the United States of America

A Special Gift for

_____

From

_____

Note

_____

_____

_____

Date

_____

God really loves you!

He loves you this much!

God is our Father in Heaven.

God made each one of us,
and we are each made special!

1 John 3:1 Behold, what manner of love the Father hath bestowed upon us, that we should be called the sons of God: therefore the world knoweth us not, because it knew him not.

Romans 8:39 Nor height, nor depth, nor any other creature, shall be able to separate us from the love of God, which is in Christ Jesus our Lord.

God
is holy and special.
He is
three persons in one:

God the Father,
God the Son, Jesus,
and
God the Holy Spirit.

1 John 5:7 For there are three that bear record in heaven, the Father, the Word, and the Holy Ghost: and these three are one.

If you tell God you are sorry for your sins, and don't want to sin, God will hear you!

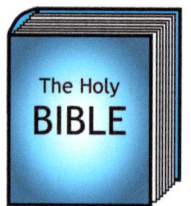

The Bible says that if you confess with your mouth and believe in your heart that God gave his son, Jesus, to die on the cross to pay for all your sins, you are saved!

You are forgiven, and you will go to heaven some day!

Jesus arose from the grave, and He is alive today, in heaven with God!

Thank you Jesus, for saving me!

John 3:16 For God so loved the world, that he gave his only begotten Son, that whosoever believeth in him should not perish, but have everlasting life.

Romans 10:9 That if thou shalt confess with thy mouth the Lord Jesus, and shalt believe in thine heart that God hath raised him from the dead, thou shalt be saved.

After you are saved, the Holy Spirit comes to indwell in your heart.

Jesus prayed to God and God sent us the Holy Spirit! We are never alone!

The Holy Spirit helps us each and every day!

The Holy Spirit comforts us, and helps us do great things for God!

Acts 2:38 Then Peter said unto them, Repent, and be baptized every one of you in the name of Jesus Christ for the remission of sins, and ye shall receive the gift of the Holy Ghost.

John 14:25-27 These things have I spoken unto you, being yet present with you. 26 But the Comforter, which is the Holy Ghost, whom the Father will send in my name, he shall teach you all things, and bring all things to your remembrance, whatsoever I have said unto you. 27 Peace I leave with you, my peace I give unto you: not as the world giveth, give I unto you. Let not your heart be troubled, neither let it be afraid.

God gave each person natural talents.
You can do a job and earn money.
You can love what you do, each day!

You might have skills to be an artist. You might be really good at playing a musical instrument.

You might be good at farming, or cooking food. You might like to build things, or repair things that break.

Ecclesiastes 5:18 Behold that which I have seen: it is good and comely for one to eat and to drink, and to enjoy the good of all his labour that he taketh under the sun all the days of his life, which God giveth him: for it is his portion.

2 Thessalonians 3:10 For even when we were with you, this we commanded you, that if any would not work, neither should he eat.

1 Thessalonians 4:11-12 And that ye study to be quiet, and to do your own business, and to work with your own hands, as we commanded you; 12 That ye may walk honestly toward them that are without, and that ye may have lack of nothing.

God also gives you special gifts. These gifts are supernatural abilities, called spiritual gifts. Spiritual gifts help Christian people, help churches big or small, and help society.

Wherever Christians are God can work through you, and help people! Every person has a spiritual gift from God!

As we get older, we learn what our gift is!

1 Corinthians 12:4-11 Now there are diversities of gifts, but the same Spirit. 5 And there are differences of administrations, but the same Lord. 6 And there are diversities of operations, but it is the same God which worketh all in all. 7 But the manifestation of the Spirit is given to every man to profit withal. 8 For to one is given by the Spirit the word of wisdom; to another the word of knowledge by the same Spirit; 9 To another faith by the same Spirit; to another the gifts of healing by the same Spirit; 10 To another the working of miracles; to another prophecy; to another discerning of spirits; to another divers kinds of tongues; to another the interpretation of tongues: 11 But all these worketh that one and the selfsame Spirit, dividing to every man severally as he will.

Each Christian has special gifts to uplift the body of Christ (believers in Jesus) and bring glory to God.

Through God's power, and Jesus' assignment of tasks for us, the Holy Spirit gives us the spiritual gifts!

Ephesians 4:7 But unto every one of us is given grace according to the measure of the gift of Christ.

1 Corinthians 2:13 Which things also we speak, not in the words which man's wisdom teacheth, but which the Holy Ghost teacheth; comparing spiritual things with spiritual.

1 Corinthians 12:27-28 Now ye are the body of Christ, and members in particular. 28 And God hath set some in the church, first apostles, secondarily prophets, thirdly teachers, after that miracles, then gifts of healings, helps, governments, diversities of tongues.

You might help start churches, or home study groups. You might have spiritual gifts to minister to others.

Do you remember the Old Testament prophets and apostles? You could be a modern day prophet or apostle!

Ephesians 4:11-12 And he gave some, apostles; and some, prophets; and some, evangelists; and some, pastors and teachers; 12 For the perfecting of the saints, for the work of the ministry, for the edifying of the body of Christ:

Acts 2:17 And it shall come to pass in the last days, saith God, I will pour out of my Spirit upon all flesh: and your sons and your daughters shall prophesy, and your young men shall see visions, and your old men shall dream dreams:

You could be an evangelist, pastor, teacher, or helper!
You could help people learn the true Word of God!

2 Timothy 4:2-5 Preach the word; be instant in season, out of season; reprove, rebuke, exhort with all longsuffering and doctrine. 3 For the time will come when they will not endure sound doctrine; but after their own lusts shall they heap to themselves teachers, having itching ears; 4 And they shall turn away their ears from the truth, and shall be turned unto fables. 5 But watch thou in all things, endure afflictions, do the work of an evangelist, make full proof of thy ministry.

God gave each of us
a purpose.

We should use our gifts!

We should live like Jesus
taught us to live, with love.

We should be patient.

2 Timothy 3:10 But thou hast fully known my doctrine, manner of life, purpose, faith, longsuffering, charity, patience,

Romans 8:28 And we know that all things work together for good to them that love God, to them who are the called according to his purpose.

Ephesians 1:11 In whom also we have obtained an inheritance, being predestinated according to the purpose of him who worketh all things after the counsel of his own will:

You might have spiritual gifts
from the Holy Spirit to motivate others.
You could be a prophet, servant, or teacher.

You could be an encourager, giver, leader, or one who shows mercy!

Romans 12:6-8 Having then gifts differing according to the grace that is given to us, whether prophecy, let us prophesy according to the proportion of faith; 7 Or ministry, let us wait on our ministering: or he that teacheth, on teaching; 8 Or he that exhorteth, on exhortation: he that giveth, let him do it with simplicity; he that ruleth, with diligence; he that sheweth mercy, with cheerfulness.

Do you remember Jesus healing people?

You could have the spiritual gifts of manifestation. You could be a person who has the gift of healing or miraculous powers. You could be a person who has wisdom, knowledge, or faith. You could be a prophet, one who speaks in tongues or interprets, or a person who discerns good from bad.

1 Corinthians 12:7-11 But the manifestation of the Spirit is given to every man to profit withal. 8 For to one is given by the Spirit the word of wisdom; to another the word of knowledge by the same Spirit; 9 To another faith by the same Spirit; to another the gifts of healing by the same Spirit; 10 To another the working of miracles; to another prophecy; to another discerning of spirits; to another divers kinds of tongues; to another the interpretation of tongues: 11 But all these worketh that one and the selfsame Spirit, dividing to every man severally as he will.

With our special
supernatural gifts
from God,
the Holy Spirit helps us
share God's love.

We can share the Gospel
(good news)
and tell people
about Jesus,
and how to be saved.

We can share the Gospel
with all creatures!

Mark 16:15 And he said unto them, Go ye into all the world, and preach the gospel to every creature.

Matthew 24:14 And this gospel of the kingdom shall be preached in all the world for a witness unto all nations; and then shall the end come.

We can do the work God has set out for us to do in our lifetime!
Pray to God to ask what your spiritual gift is.

As people, we are known by the good things we do. Spiritual gifts help us show God's love and bring glory to Him.

We love others because God loved us first!

1 Timothy 4:14 The existence of a gift is a call to exercise it. Paul advised Timothy, "Neglect not the gift that is in you,"

Matthew 7:16 But, Jesus said: "For by their fruit you shall know them"

2 Timothy 1:9 Who hath saved us, and called us with an holy calling, not according to our works, but according to his own purpose and grace, which was given us in Christ Jesus before the world began,

Love not the world,
nor the things that are in the world.

Serve God, not money.

1 John 2:15-16 Love not the world,
neither the things that are in the world.
If any man love the world, the love of the Father is not in him. 16 For all that is in the world, the lust of the flesh, and the lust of the eyes, and the pride of life, is not of the Father, but is of the world.

Matthew 6:24 No man can serve two masters: for either he will hate the one, and love the other; or else he will hold to the one, and despise the other.
Ye cannot serve God and mammon.

We might have the gift of discernment to know if there is a spirit of good or evil.

We should not be jealous of anyone else's gift.

We should have joy, and love one another!

Have great faith in God!

Hebrews 5:14 But strong meat belongeth to them that are of full age, even those who by reason of use have their senses exercised to discern both good and evil.

Galatians 5:22-26 But the fruit of the Spirit is love, joy, peace, longsuffering, gentleness, goodness, faith, 23 Meekness, temperance: against such there is no law. 24 And they that are Christ's have crucified the flesh with the affections and lusts. 25 If we live in the Spirit, let us also walk in the Spirit. 26 Let us not be desirous of vain glory, provoking one another, envying one another.

Study the Bible every day!
Pray to God each day! Show love to everyone.

Obey God. We want to please Him. God loves us!

2 Timothy 2:15 Study to shew thyself approved unto God, a workman that needeth not to be ashamed, rightly dividing the word of truth.

Jeremiah 7:23 But this thing commanded I them, saying, Obey my voice, and I will be your God, and ye shall be my people: and walk ye in all the ways that I have commanded you, that it may be well unto you.

Matthew 22:37-39 Jesus said unto him, Thou shalt love the Lord thy God with all thy heart, and with all thy soul, and with all thy mind. 38 This is the first and great commandment. 39 And the second is like unto it, Thou shalt love thy neighbour as thyself.

You have natural talents and spiritual gifts from God. God has blessed you!
Work hard, and enjoy life!

Don't do bad things. Fight the good fight for your Father in Heaven. Use your gifts!

1 Timothy 6:12 *Fight the good fight of faith, lay hold on eternal life, whereunto thou art also called, and hast professed a good profession before many witnesses.*

2 Timothy 2:3-5 *Thou therefore endure hardness, as a good soldier of Jesus Christ. 4 No man that warreth entangleth himself with the affairs of this life; that he may please him who hath chosen him to be a soldier. 5 And if a man also strive for masteries, yet is he not crowned, except he strive lawfully.*

James 1:12 *Blessed is the man that endureth temptation: for when he is tried, he shall receive the crown of life, which the Lord hath promised to them that love him.*

God loves you! Be happy knowing this!
You can feel intense joy!

Look around you, to see the good things. Feel inspired by all the good things God has made, until Jesus returns!

Know that one day you will spend eternity with God, Jesus and the Holy Spirit!

When we all get to heaven, it will be wonderful! Until then, we use our special spiritual gifts to bring glory to God!

Acts 2:28 Thou hast made known to me the ways of life; thou shalt make me full of joy with thy countenance.

Romans 15:13 Now the God of hope fill you with all joy and peace in believing, that ye may abound in hope, through the power of the Holy Ghost.

John 14:1-4 Let not your heart be troubled: ye believe in God, believe also in me. 2 In my Father's house are many mansions: if it were not so, I would have told you. I go to prepare a place for you. 3 And if I go and prepare a place for you, I will come again, and receive you unto myself; that where I am, there ye may be also. 4 And whither I go ye know, and the way ye know.

Jesus loves you! God gives special gifts to you! The Holy Spirit is always with you!

2 Timothy 1:6-9 Wherefore I put thee in remembrance that thou stir up the gift of God, which is in thee by the putting on of my hands. 7 For God hath not given us the spirit of fear; but of power, and of love, and of a sound mind. 8 Be not thou therefore ashamed of the testimony of our Lord, nor of me his prisoner: but be thou partaker of the afflictions of the gospel according to the power of God; 9 Who hath saved us, and called us with an holy calling, not according to our works, but according to his own purpose and grace, which was given us in Christ Jesus before the world began,

God Really Loves You Book Series™

GodReallyLovesYou.com

1 Corinthians 12:4-7 Now there are diversities of gifts, but the same Spirit. 5 And there are differences of administrations, but the same Lord. 6 And there are diversities of operations, but it is the same God which worketh all in all. 7 But the manifestation of the Spirit is given to every man to profit withal.

Matthew 18:3-5 And said, Verily I say unto you, Except ye be converted, and become as little children, ye shall not enter into the kingdom of heaven. 4 Whosoever therefore shall humble himself as this little child, the same is greatest in the kingdom of heaven. 5 And whoso shall receive one such little child in my name receiveth me.

www.ingramcontent.com/pod-product-compliance
Lightning Source LLC
LaVergne TN
LVHW070433080526
838201LV00128B/263